Sex

Strong
and Weak

About Starters Science books

STARTERS SCIENCE books are designed to encourage scientific awareness in young children. The series aims to focus the instinctive curiosity of children and to encourage exploration and experiment. It also aims to develop language, encourage discussion and suggest situations where children can examine similarities and differences.

The text of each book is simple enough for children to read for themselves, and the vocabulary has been controlled to ensure that about 90 per cent of the words used will be familiar to them. Each book also contains a picture index and a page of notes for parents and teachers.

Written and planned by Albert James
Illustrator: Robin Anderson

A MACDONALD BOOK

© Macdonald & Co (Publishers) Ltd 1973

First published in
Great Britain in 1973

Reprinted 1974, 1983 and 1986

Printed and bound in Great Britain by
Hazell, Watson & Viney Ltd
Aylesbury, Buckinghamshire

Published by Macdonald & Co (Publishers) Ltd
Greater London House
Hampstead Road
London NW1 7QX

Members of BPCC plc

British Library Cataloguing in Publication Data
James, Albert
Strong and weak. — (Starters science)
  1. Readers — 1950 —
  I. Title II. Series
  428.6   PE1119

  ISBN 0-356-05134-X
  ISBN 0-356-09277-1 Pbk

STARTERS
SCIENCE

Strong
and Weak

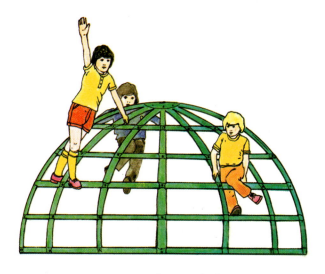

Macdonald

Look at the strong man.
He can lift heavy weights.
He has big muscles.

2

Test how strong you are.
How long can you hold up a stool
with one hand?
Which of your muscles get tired?

These animals are strong.
An ant is small, but it can lift loads
as heavy as its own body.

4

Trees are strong plants.
Wood from trees is used for building.
Look at these roof timbers.

5

Strips of paper are not very strong.
You can cut them and bend them.
See what you can build
with strips of paper.

6

Fold some strips longways.
Now they are stronger.
Can you build a higher model?

7

Put a piece of card on two bricks.
Does the card sag when you put
a small weight on it?
Fold up the edges of the card.
Is it any stronger?
8

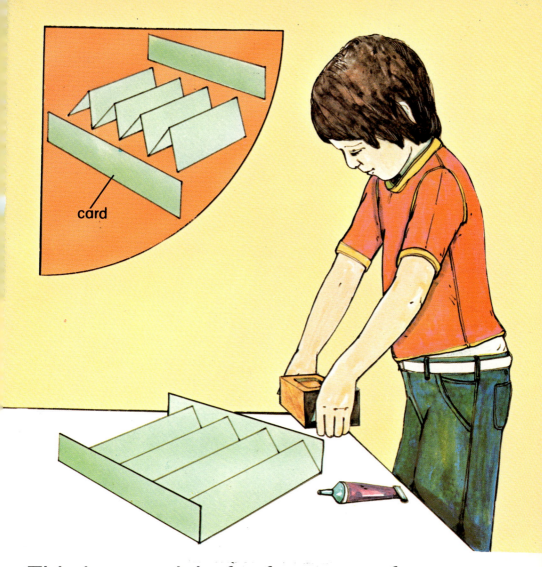

card

This is a model of a factory roof.
Glue the sides on firmly.
Put a brick on top to test it.
Is it a strong shape?

flour and water paste

bricks

Paste sheets of newspaper together.
Let them dry to form stiff boards.
How many sheets thick must they be
to carry your weight?

10

Make tubes from sheets of newspaper.
Roll each sheet round a stick.
Fix it with sticky tape
and slide out the stick.
What can you build with these tubes?

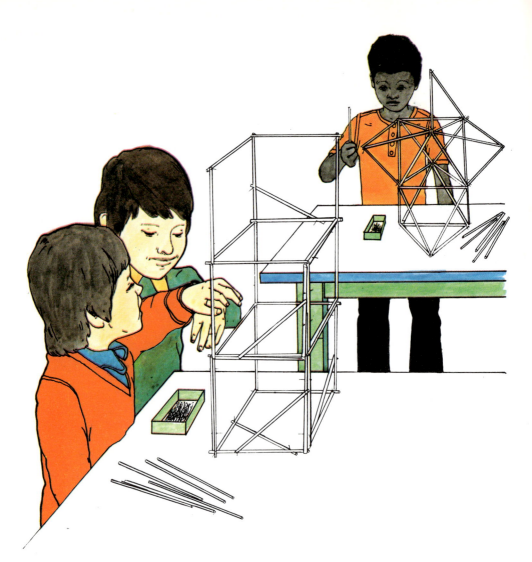

Build a high tower with drinking straws.
Fix the straws together with pins.
Ask a grown-up to help you.
Put the pins away afterwards.

12

Tubes are good for building
because they are strong and light.
This swimming pool has a roof
built of tubes.

drinking
straws

How many spoons of sand
will bend one straw?
Try two straws together.
Try different numbers of straws.
14

newspaper tubes

weights

Make a bundle of paper tubes.
Test how strong it is.

15

different glues

glue together

pieces of wood

marbles

Find some different kinds of glue.
Test how strong they are like this.
How many marbles are needed
to break the joint?

16

one weight

three weights

five weights

You can test these cardboard bridges.
Put small weights in the middle.
Arches are strong shapes.

17

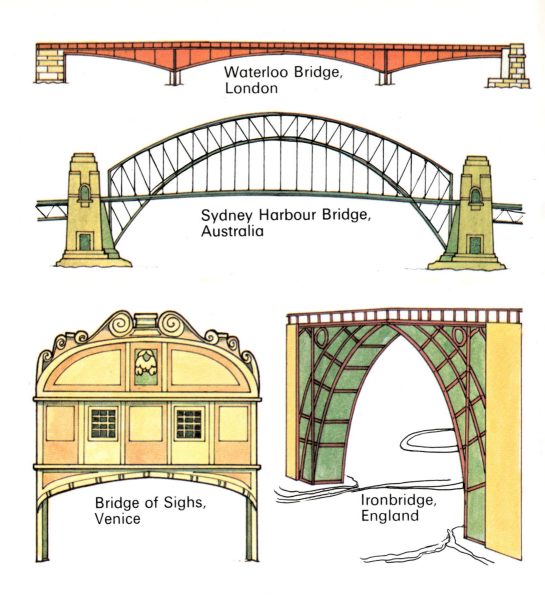

Waterloo Bridge,
London

Sydney Harbour Bridge,
Australia

Bridge of Sighs,
Venice

Ironbridge,
England

These are some famous bridges.
Look at the different arches.

18

Look for bridges with arches
where you live.
Have they got big arches or small ones?

19

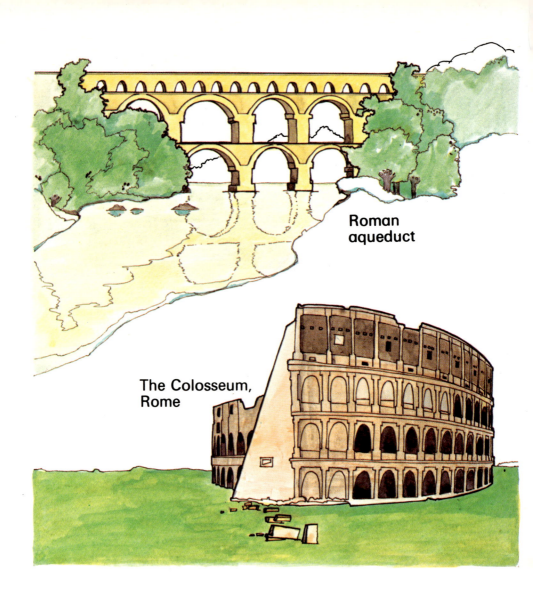

Roman
aqueduct

The Colosseum,
Rome

The Romans built these arches
long ago.

20

Look for arches in buildings.
Look at old buildings and new ones.

Make these frameworks out of card.
One of them is strong and firm.
Which one is it?

22

Look at these strong framework shapes.
They are used in many structures.

Many bridges have strong steel
frameworks.

24

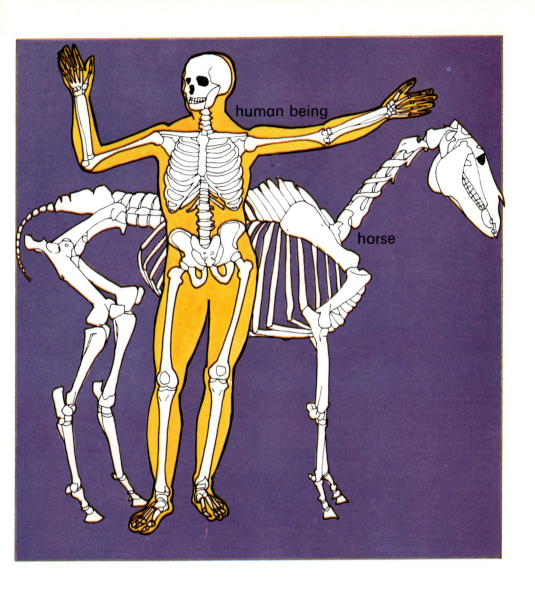

Human beings and most animals
have a strong framework made of bones.
It is called a skeleton.

Spiders spin a strong thread.
Strong wires and ropes are spun
by twisting lots of threads together.
What are they used for?

26

This bridge is called a suspension bridge.
Strong cables hold it up.
The cables are made of hundreds
of steel wires spun together.

27

Index

weights
(page 2)

muscles
(page 2)

news-paper
(page 10)

tubes
(page 11)

drinking straws
(page 12)

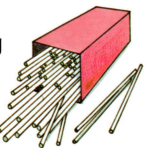

bundle
(page 15)

joint
(page 16)

arch
(page 17)

framework
(page 22)

skeleton
(page 25)

Notes for Parents and Teachers

Starters Science books are designed for children to read and study on their own, but children would also benefit by sharing these topics with a parent or teacher. These brief notes explain the scientific ideas contained in the book, and help the interested adult to expand the themes.

2–4   The strength of human beings and other animals is illustrated and compared.

5   Children are introduced to the idea that trees are the strongest plants, and that we obtain wood, a strong material, from them.

6–9   By means of simple experiments, children can discover that the shape of a material affects its strength.

10   Children can find out how many thicknesses of newspaper, glued together, will carry their own weight.

11–13   These simple experiments help children to find out that tubes are light and strong, and are therefore very useful for building.

14–15   Children can discover that by combining tubes into a bundle, their strength is increased.

16   Children are encouraged to test the strengths of different kinds of glues.

17–21   These pages encourage children to observe that an arch shape is strong, and that arches are often used in bridges and other buildings. Ancient and modern arches are illustrated.

22–25   Frameworks are examined. Children are shown how to make a rigid framework, and the use of frameworks in engineering is illustrated. Children can also see how the structure of many animals is based on a framework of bones.

26   The varied uses of different kinds of ropes, wires and threads are illustrated.

27   Children are shown that the cables which support a suspension bridge are formed from hundreds of steel wires in a bundle.